THE CAREGIVER'S GUIDE TO STRICT AND LOVING DISCIPLINE

The Tools You Need to Give a Spanking by the Book!

By Clarine Klein, Professor of Spankology

OFFICIAL
SPANKING DIARY

ISBN: 979-8-9857980-1-2
Imprint: Studio Bebop Inc.

Cover Illustration by Arkham-Insanity
https://www.patreon.com/isadoraarkham
https://twitter.com/ArkhamInsanity

This book is a work of fiction. Activities represented in this book are fantasies only.

This Spanking Diary belongs to

_____

I am a

☐ Little   ☐ Middle

My Caregiver is my

☐ Mommy   ☐ Daddy   ☐ Parent
☐ Aunt   ☐ Uncle   ☐ Relative
☐ Grandma   ☐ Grandpa   ☐ Grandparent
☐ Older Sister ☐ Older Brother ☐ Sibling
☐ Nanny   ☐ Babysitter   ☐ Teacher

_____

My other Caregiver is my

☐ Mommy   ☐ Daddy   ☐ Parent
☐ Aunt   ☐ Uncle   ☐ Relative
☐ Grandma   ☐ Grandpa   ☐ Grandparent
☐ Older Sister ☐ Older Brother ☐ Sibling
☐ Nanny   ☐ Babysitter   ☐ Teacher

_____

My Behavior Contract

I promise to

_____

_____

_____

_____

_____

Our House Rules are

_____

_____

_____

_____

_____

When I behave myself, my Caregiver(s) promise to

_____

_____

_____

_____

I understand the rules above and I promise to obey. I understand that when I behave well I will receive a reward, but I also agree that if I misbehave I will be spanked as a punishment.

My Signature _____

Caregiver's Signature _____

Spanking Report

Date _____ / _____ / _____

Today I was spanked by _____

I was spanked because I

_____

_____

What I did was wrong because

_____

_____

I was spanked on my

- ☐ Panties
- ☐ Underwear
- ☐ Diaper
- ☐ Pull-up
- ☐ Bare Bottom

I was spanked

- ☐ Over the Knee
- ☐ Bending Over
- ☐ Lying Face Down
- ☐ Diaper Position
- ☐ _____

I was spanked with a

- ☐ Hand
- ☐ Hairbrush
- ☐ Bath Brush
- ☐ Paddle
- ☐ Wooden Spoon
- ☐ Slipper
- ☐ Cane
- ☐ Switch
- ☐ Belt
- ☐ Leather Strap
- ☐ Tawse
- ☐ _____

Next time I will

_____

_____

Caregiver's Signature _____

Spanking Report

Date _____ / _____ / _____

Today I was spanked by _____

I was spanked because I

_____

_____

What I did was wrong because

_____

_____

I was spanked on my

- ☐ Panties
- ☐ Underwear
- ☐ Diaper
- ☐ Pull-up
- ☐ Bare Bottom

I was spanked

- ☐ Over the Knee
- ☐ Bending Over
- ☐ Lying Face Down
- ☐ Diaper Position
- ☐ _____

I was spanked with a

- ☐ Hand
- ☐ Hairbrush
- ☐ Bath Brush
- ☐ Paddle
- ☐ Wooden Spoon
- ☐ Slipper
- ☐ Cane
- ☐ Switch
- ☐ Belt
- ☐ Leather Strap
- ☐ Tawse
- ☐ _____

Next time I will

_____

_____

Caregiver's Signature _____

Spanking Report

Date _____ / _____ / _____

Today I was spanked by _____

I was spanked because I

_____

_____

What I did was wrong because

_____

_____

I was spanked on my

- ☐ Panties
- ☐ Underwear
- ☐ Diaper
- ☐ Pull-up
- ☐ Bare Bottom

I was spanked

- ☐ Over the Knee
- ☐ Bending Over
- ☐ Lying Face Down
- ☐ Diaper Position
- ☐ _____

I was spanked with a

- ☐ Hand
- ☐ Hairbrush
- ☐ Bath Brush
- ☐ Paddle
- ☐ Wooden Spoon
- ☐ Slipper
- ☐ Cane
- ☐ Switch
- ☐ Belt
- ☐ Leather Strap
- ☐ Tawse
- ☐ _____

Next time I will

_____

_____

Caregiver's Signature _____

Spanking Report

Date _____ / _____ / _____

Today I was spanked by _____

I was spanked because I

_____

_____

What I did was wrong because

_____

_____

I was spanked on my

☐ Panties   ☐ Diaper   ☐ Bare Bottom

☐ Underwear   ☐ Pull-up

I was spanked

☐ Over the Knee   ☐ Lying Face Down   ☐ _____

☐ Bending Over   ☐ Diaper Position

I was spanked with a

☐ Hand   ☐ Wooden Spoon   ☐ Belt

☐ Hairbrush   ☐ Slipper   ☐ Leather Strap

☐ Bath Brush   ☐ Cane   ☐ Tawse

☐ Paddle   ☐ Switch   ☐ _____

Next time I will

_____

_____

Caregiver's Signature _____

Spanking Report

Date ____ / ____ / ____

Today I was spanked by _____

I was spanked because I

_____

_____

What I did was wrong because

_____

_____

I was spanked on my

- ☐ Panties
- ☐ Diaper
- ☐ Bare Bottom
- ☐ Underwear
- ☐ Pull-up

I was spanked

- ☐ Over the Knee
- ☐ Lying Face Down
- ☐ _____
- ☐ Bending Over
- ☐ Diaper Position

I was spanked with a

- ☐ Hand
- ☐ Wooden Spoon
- ☐ Belt
- ☐ Hairbrush
- ☐ Slipper
- ☐ Leather Strap
- ☐ Bath Brush
- ☐ Cane
- ☐ Tawse
- ☐ Paddle
- ☐ Switch
- ☐ _____

Next time I will

_____

_____

Caregiver's Signature _____

Spanking Report

Date _____ / _____ / _____

Today I was spanked by _____

I was spanked because I

_____

_____

What I did was wrong because

_____

_____

I was spanked on my

- ☐ Panties   ☐ Diaper   ☐ Bare Bottom
- ☐ Underwear   ☐ Pull-up

I was spanked

- ☐ Over the Knee   ☐ Lying Face Down   ☐ _____
- ☐ Bending Over   ☐ Diaper Position

I was spanked with a

- ☐ Hand   ☐ Wooden Spoon   ☐ Belt
- ☐ Hairbrush   ☐ Slipper   ☐ Leather Strap
- ☐ Bath Brush   ☐ Cane   ☐ Tawse
- ☐ Paddle   ☐ Switch   ☐ _____

Next time I will

_____

_____

Caregiver's Signature _____

Spanking Report

Date _____ / _____ / _____

Today I was spanked by _____

I was spanked because I

_____

_____

What I did was wrong because

_____

_____

I was spanked on my

☐ Panties   ☐ Diaper   ☐ Bare Bottom

☐ Underwear   ☐ Pull-up

I was spanked

☐ Over the Knee   ☐ Lying Face Down   ☐ _____

☐ Bending Over   ☐ Diaper Position

I was spanked with a

☐ Hand   ☐ Wooden Spoon   ☐ Belt

☐ Hairbrush   ☐ Slipper   ☐ Leather Strap

☐ Bath Brush ☐ Cane   ☐ Tawse

☐ Paddle   ☐ Switch   ☐ _____

Next time I will

_____

_____

Caregiver's Signature _____

Spanking Report

Date _____ / _____ / _____

Today I was spanked by _____

I was spanked because I

_____

_____

What I did was wrong because

_____

_____

I was spanked on my

- ☐ Panties
- ☐ Underwear
- ☐ Diaper
- ☐ Pull-up
- ☐ Bare Bottom

I was spanked

- ☐ Over the Knee
- ☐ Bending Over
- ☐ Lying Face Down
- ☐ Diaper Position
- ☐ _____

I was spanked with a

- ☐ Hand
- ☐ Hairbrush
- ☐ Bath Brush
- ☐ Paddle
- ☐ Wooden Spoon
- ☐ Slipper
- ☐ Cane
- ☐ Switch
- ☐ Belt
- ☐ Leather Strap
- ☐ Tawse
- ☐ _____

Next time I will

_____

_____

Caregiver's Signature _____

Spanking Report

Date _____ / _____ / _____

Today I was spanked by _____

I was spanked because I

_____

_____

What I did was wrong because

_____

_____

I was spanked on my

☐ Panties ☐ Diaper ☐ Bare Bottom

☐ Underwear ☐ Pull-up

I was spanked

☐ Over the Knee ☐ Lying Face Down ☐ _____

☐ Bending Over ☐ Diaper Position

I was spanked with a

☐ Hand ☐ Wooden Spoon ☐ Belt

☐ Hairbrush ☐ Slipper ☐ Leather Strap

☐ Bath Brush ☐ Cane ☐ Tawse

☐ Paddle ☐ Switch ☐ _____

Next time I will

_____

_____

Caregiver's Signature _____

Spanking Report

Date _____ / _____ / _____

Today I was spanked by _____

I was spanked because I

_____

_____

What I did was wrong because

_____

_____

I was spanked on my

- ☐ Panties
- ☐ Diaper
- ☐ Bare Bottom
- ☐ Underwear
- ☐ Pull-up

I was spanked

- ☐ Over the Knee
- ☐ Lying Face Down
- ☐ _____
- ☐ Bending Over
- ☐ Diaper Position

I was spanked with a

- ☐ Hand
- ☐ Wooden Spoon
- ☐ Belt
- ☐ Hairbrush
- ☐ Slipper
- ☐ Leather Strap
- ☐ Bath Brush
- ☐ Cane
- ☐ Tawse
- ☐ Paddle
- ☐ Switch
- ☐ _____

Next time I will

_____

_____

Caregiver's Signature _____

Spanking Report

Date _____ / _____ / _____

Today I was spanked by _____

I was spanked because I

_____

_____

What I did was wrong because

_____

_____

I was spanked on my

- ☐ Panties
- ☐ Underwear
- ☐ Diaper
- ☐ Pull-up
- ☐ Bare Bottom

I was spanked

- ☐ Over the Knee
- ☐ Bending Over
- ☐ Lying Face Down
- ☐ Diaper Position
- ☐ _____

I was spanked with a

- ☐ Hand
- ☐ Hairbrush
- ☐ Bath Brush
- ☐ Paddle
- ☐ Wooden Spoon
- ☐ Slipper
- ☐ Cane
- ☐ Switch
- ☐ Belt
- ☐ Leather Strap
- ☐ Tawse
- ☐ _____

Next time I will

_____

_____

Caregiver's Signature _____

Spanking Report

Date _____ / _____ / _____

Today I was spanked by _____

I was spanked because I

_____

_____

What I did was wrong because

_____

_____

I was spanked on my

☐ Panties   ☐ Diaper   ☐ Bare Bottom

☐ Underwear   ☐ Pull-up

I was spanked

☐ Over the Knee   ☐ Lying Face Down   ☐ _____

☐ Bending Over   ☐ Diaper Position

I was spanked with a

☐ Hand   ☐ Wooden Spoon   ☐ Belt

☐ Hairbrush   ☐ Slipper   ☐ Leather Strap

☐ Bath Brush   ☐ Cane   ☐ Tawse

☐ Paddle   ☐ Switch   ☐ _____

Next time I will

_____

_____

Caregiver's Signature _____

Spanking Report

Date _____ / _____ / _____

Today I was spanked by _____

I was spanked because I

_____

_____

What I did was wrong because

_____

_____

I was spanked on my

☐ Panties   ☐ Diaper   ☐ Bare Bottom

☐ Underwear   ☐ Pull-up

I was spanked

☐ Over the Knee   ☐ Lying Face Down   ☐ _____

☐ Bending Over   ☐ Diaper Position

I was spanked with a

☐ Hand   ☐ Wooden Spoon   ☐ Belt

☐ Hairbrush   ☐ Slipper   ☐ Leather Strap

☐ Bath Brush   ☐ Cane   ☐ Tawse

☐ Paddle   ☐ Switch   ☐ _____

Next time I will

_____

_____

Caregiver's Signature _____

Spanking Report

Date ____ /____ /____

Today I was spanked by _____

I was spanked because I

_____

_____

What I did was wrong because

_____

_____

I was spanked on my

- ☐ Panties
- ☐ Underwear
- ☐ Diaper
- ☐ Pull-up
- ☐ Bare Bottom

I was spanked

- ☐ Over the Knee
- ☐ Bending Over
- ☐ Lying Face Down
- ☐ Diaper Position
- ☐ _____

I was spanked with a

- ☐ Hand
- ☐ Hairbrush
- ☐ Bath Brush
- ☐ Paddle
- ☐ Wooden Spoon
- ☐ Slipper
- ☐ Cane
- ☐ Switch
- ☐ Belt
- ☐ Leather Strap
- ☐ Tawse
- ☐ _____

Next time I will

_____

_____

Caregiver's Signature _____

Spanking Report

Date ____ / ____ / ____

Today I was spanked by _____

I was spanked because I

_____

_____

What I did was wrong because

_____

_____

I was spanked on my

- ☐ Panties
- ☐ Underwear
- ☐ Diaper
- ☐ Pull-up
- ☐ Bare Bottom

I was spanked

- ☐ Over the Knee
- ☐ Bending Over
- ☐ Lying Face Down
- ☐ Diaper Position
- ☐ _____

I was spanked with a

- ☐ Hand
- ☐ Hairbrush
- ☐ Bath Brush
- ☐ Paddle
- ☐ Wooden Spoon
- ☐ Slipper
- ☐ Cane
- ☐ Switch
- ☐ Belt
- ☐ Leather Strap
- ☐ Tawse
- ☐ _____

Next time I will

_____

_____

Caregiver's Signature _____

Spanking Report

Date ____ / ____ / ____

Today I was spanked by _____

I was spanked because I

_____

_____

What I did was wrong because

_____

_____

I was spanked on my

- ☐ Panties
- ☐ Underwear
- ☐ Diaper
- ☐ Pull-up
- ☐ Bare Bottom

I was spanked

- ☐ Over the Knee
- ☐ Bending Over
- ☐ Lying Face Down
- ☐ Diaper Position
- ☐ _____

I was spanked with a

- ☐ Hand
- ☐ Hairbrush
- ☐ Bath Brush
- ☐ Paddle
- ☐ Wooden Spoon
- ☐ Slipper
- ☐ Cane
- ☐ Switch
- ☐ Belt
- ☐ Leather Strap
- ☐ Tawse
- ☐ _____

Next time I will

_____

_____

Caregiver's Signature _____

Spanking Report

Date _____ / _____ / _____

Today I was spanked by _____

I was spanked because I

_____

_____

What I did was wrong because

_____

_____

I was spanked on my

- ☐ Panties
- ☐ Underwear
- ☐ Diaper
- ☐ Pull-up
- ☐ Bare Bottom

I was spanked

- ☐ Over the Knee
- ☐ Bending Over
- ☐ Lying Face Down
- ☐ Diaper Position
- ☐ _____

I was spanked with a

- ☐ Hand
- ☐ Hairbrush
- ☐ Bath Brush
- ☐ Paddle
- ☐ Wooden Spoon
- ☐ Slipper
- ☐ Cane
- ☐ Switch
- ☐ Belt
- ☐ Leather Strap
- ☐ Tawse
- ☐ _____

Next time I will

_____

_____

Caregiver's Signature _____

Spanking Report

Date _____ / _____ / _____

Today I was spanked by _____

I was spanked because I

_____

_____

What I did was wrong because

_____

_____

I was spanked on my

- ☐ Panties
- ☐ Underwear
- ☐ Diaper
- ☐ Pull-up
- ☐ Bare Bottom

I was spanked

- ☐ Over the Knee
- ☐ Bending Over
- ☐ Lying Face Down
- ☐ Diaper Position
- ☐ _____

I was spanked with a

- ☐ Hand
- ☐ Hairbrush
- ☐ Bath Brush
- ☐ Paddle
- ☐ Wooden Spoon
- ☐ Slipper
- ☐ Cane
- ☐ Switch
- ☐ Belt
- ☐ Leather Strap
- ☐ Tawse
- ☐ _____

Next time I will

_____

_____

Caregiver's Signature _____

Spanking Report

Date ____ / ____ / ____

Today I was spanked by _____

I was spanked because I

_____

_____

What I did was wrong because

_____

_____

I was spanked on my

- ☐ Panties
- ☐ Underwear
- ☐ Diaper
- ☐ Pull-up
- ☐ Bare Bottom

I was spanked

- ☐ Over the Knee
- ☐ Bending Over
- ☐ Lying Face Down
- ☐ Diaper Position
- ☐ _____

I was spanked with a

- ☐ Hand
- ☐ Hairbrush
- ☐ Bath Brush
- ☐ Paddle
- ☐ Wooden Spoon
- ☐ Slipper
- ☐ Cane
- ☐ Switch
- ☐ Belt
- ☐ Leather Strap
- ☐ Tawse
- ☐ _____

Next time I will

_____

_____

Caregiver's Signature _____

Spanking Report

Date _____ / _____ / _____

Today I was spanked by _____

I was spanked because I

_____

_____

What I did was wrong because

_____

_____

I was spanked on my

- ☐ Panties
- ☐ Underwear
- ☐ Diaper
- ☐ Pull-up
- ☐ Bare Bottom

I was spanked

- ☐ Over the Knee
- ☐ Bending Over
- ☐ Lying Face Down
- ☐ Diaper Position
- ☐ _____

I was spanked with a

- ☐ Hand
- ☐ Hairbrush
- ☐ Bath Brush
- ☐ Paddle
- ☐ Wooden Spoon
- ☐ Slipper
- ☐ Cane
- ☐ Switch
- ☐ Belt
- ☐ Leather Strap
- ☐ Tawse
- ☐ _____

Next time I will

_____

_____

Caregiver's Signature _____

Spanking Report

Date ____ / ____ / ____

Today I was spanked by _____

I was spanked because I

_____

_____

What I did was wrong because

_____

_____

I was spanked on my

☐ Panties   ☐ Diaper   ☐ Bare Bottom

☐ Underwear   ☐ Pull-up

I was spanked

☐ Over the Knee   ☐ Lying Face Down   ☐ _____

☐ Bending Over   ☐ Diaper Position

I was spanked with a

☐ Hand   ☐ Wooden Spoon   ☐ Belt

☐ Hairbrush   ☐ Slipper   ☐ Leather Strap

☐ Bath Brush   ☐ Cane   ☐ Tawse

☐ Paddle   ☐ Switch   ☐ _____

Next time I will

_____

_____

Caregiver's Signature _____

Spanking Report

Date _____ / _____ / _____

Today I was spanked by _____

I was spanked because I

_____

_____

What I did was wrong because

_____

_____

I was spanked on my

- ☐ Panties
- ☐ Underwear
- ☐ Diaper
- ☐ Pull-up
- ☐ Bare Bottom

I was spanked

- ☐ Over the Knee
- ☐ Bending Over
- ☐ Lying Face Down
- ☐ Diaper Position
- ☐ _____

I was spanked with a

- ☐ Hand
- ☐ Hairbrush
- ☐ Bath Brush
- ☐ Paddle
- ☐ Wooden Spoon
- ☐ Slipper
- ☐ Cane
- ☐ Switch
- ☐ Belt
- ☐ Leather Strap
- ☐ Tawse
- ☐ _____

Next time I will

_____

_____

Caregiver's Signature _____

Spanking Report

Date ____ / ____ / ____

Today I was spanked by _____

I was spanked because I

_____

_____

What I did was wrong because

_____

_____

I was spanked on my

- ☐ Panties
- ☐ Underwear
- ☐ Diaper
- ☐ Pull-up
- ☐ Bare Bottom

I was spanked

- ☐ Over the Knee
- ☐ Bending Over
- ☐ Lying Face Down
- ☐ Diaper Position
- ☐ _____

I was spanked with a

- ☐ Hand
- ☐ Hairbrush
- ☐ Bath Brush
- ☐ Paddle
- ☐ Wooden Spoon
- ☐ Slipper
- ☐ Cane
- ☐ Switch
- ☐ Belt
- ☐ Leather Strap
- ☐ Tawse
- ☐ _____

Next time I will

_____

_____

Caregiver's Signature _____

Spanking Report

Date _____ / _____ / _____

Today I was spanked by _____

I was spanked because I

_____

_____

What I did was wrong because

_____

_____

I was spanked on my

- ☐ Panties
- ☐ Underwear
- ☐ Diaper
- ☐ Pull-up
- ☐ Bare Bottom

I was spanked

- ☐ Over the Knee
- ☐ Bending Over
- ☐ Lying Face Down
- ☐ Diaper Position
- ☐ _____

I was spanked with a

- ☐ Hand
- ☐ Hairbrush
- ☐ Bath Brush
- ☐ Paddle
- ☐ Wooden Spoon
- ☐ Slipper
- ☐ Cane
- ☐ Switch
- ☐ Belt
- ☐ Leather Strap
- ☐ Tawse
- ☐ _____

Next time I will

_____

_____

Caregiver's Signature _____

Spanking Report

Date _____ / _____ / _____

Today I was spanked by _____

I was spanked because I

_____

_____

What I did was wrong because

_____

_____

I was spanked on my

- ☐ Panties
- ☐ Underwear
- ☐ Diaper
- ☐ Pull-up
- ☐ Bare Bottom

I was spanked

- ☐ Over the Knee
- ☐ Bending Over
- ☐ Lying Face Down
- ☐ Diaper Position
- ☐ _____

I was spanked with a

- ☐ Hand
- ☐ Hairbrush
- ☐ Bath Brush
- ☐ Paddle
- ☐ Wooden Spoon
- ☐ Slipper
- ☐ Cane
- ☐ Switch
- ☐ Belt
- ☐ Leather Strap
- ☐ Tawse
- ☐ _____

Next time I will

_____

_____

Caregiver's Signature _____

Spanking Report

Date _____ / _____ / _____

Today I was spanked by _____

I was spanked because I

_____

_____

What I did was wrong because

_____

_____

I was spanked on my

- ☐ Panties
- ☐ Underwear
- ☐ Diaper
- ☐ Pull-up
- ☐ Bare Bottom

I was spanked

- ☐ Over the Knee
- ☐ Bending Over
- ☐ Lying Face Down
- ☐ Diaper Position
- ☐ _____

I was spanked with a

- ☐ Hand
- ☐ Hairbrush
- ☐ Bath Brush
- ☐ Paddle
- ☐ Wooden Spoon
- ☐ Slipper
- ☐ Cane
- ☐ Switch
- ☐ Belt
- ☐ Leather Strap
- ☐ Tawse
- ☐ _____

Next time I will

_____

_____

Caregiver's Signature _____

Spanking Report

Date ____ / ____ / ____

Today I was spanked by _____

I was spanked because I

_____

_____

What I did was wrong because

_____

_____

I was spanked on my

☐ Panties ☐ Diaper ☐ Bare Bottom
☐ Underwear ☐ Pull-up

I was spanked

☐ Over the Knee ☐ Lying Face Down ☐ _____
☐ Bending Over ☐ Diaper Position

I was spanked with a

☐ Hand ☐ Wooden Spoon ☐ Belt
☐ Hairbrush ☐ Slipper ☐ Leather Strap
☐ Bath Brush ☐ Cane ☐ Tawse
☐ Paddle ☐ Switch ☐ _____

Next time I will

_____

_____

Caregiver's Signature _____

Spanking Report

Date ____ / ____ / ____

Today I was spanked by _____

I was spanked because I

_____

_____

What I did was wrong because

_____

_____

I was spanked on my

- ☐ Panties
- ☐ Underwear
- ☐ Diaper
- ☐ Pull-up
- ☐ Bare Bottom

I was spanked

- ☐ Over the Knee
- ☐ Bending Over
- ☐ Lying Face Down
- ☐ Diaper Position
- ☐ _____

I was spanked with a

- ☐ Hand
- ☐ Hairbrush
- ☐ Bath Brush
- ☐ Paddle
- ☐ Wooden Spoon
- ☐ Slipper
- ☐ Cane
- ☐ Switch
- ☐ Belt
- ☐ Leather Strap
- ☐ Tawse
- ☐ _____

Next time I will

_____

_____

Caregiver's Signature _____

Spanking Report

Date _____ / _____ / _____

Today I was spanked by _____

I was spanked because I

_____

_____

What I did was wrong because

_____

_____

I was spanked on my

- ☐ Panties
- ☐ Underwear
- ☐ Diaper
- ☐ Pull-up
- ☐ Bare Bottom

I was spanked

- ☐ Over the Knee
- ☐ Bending Over
- ☐ Lying Face Down
- ☐ Diaper Position
- ☐ _____

I was spanked with a

- ☐ Hand
- ☐ Hairbrush
- ☐ Bath Brush
- ☐ Paddle
- ☐ Wooden Spoon
- ☐ Slipper
- ☐ Cane
- ☐ Switch
- ☐ Belt
- ☐ Leather Strap
- ☐ Tawse
- ☐ _____

Next time I will

_____

_____

Caregiver's Signature _____

Spanking Report

Date _____ / _____ / _____

Today I was spanked by _____

I was spanked because I

_____

_____

What I did was wrong because

_____

_____

I was spanked on my

☐ Panties   ☐ Diaper   ☐ Bare Bottom

☐ Underwear   ☐ Pull-up

I was spanked

☐ Over the Knee   ☐ Lying Face Down   ☐ _____

☐ Bending Over   ☐ Diaper Position

I was spanked with a

☐ Hand   ☐ Wooden Spoon   ☐ Belt

☐ Hairbrush   ☐ Slipper   ☐ Leather Strap

☐ Bath Brush   ☐ Cane   ☐ Tawse

☐ Paddle   ☐ Switch   ☐ _____

Next time I will

_____

_____

Caregiver's Signature _____

Spanking Report

Date ____ / ____ / ____

Today I was spanked by _____

I was spanked because I

_____

_____

What I did was wrong because

_____

_____

I was spanked on my

- ☐ Panties
- ☐ Underwear
- ☐ Diaper
- ☐ Pull-up
- ☐ Bare Bottom

I was spanked

- ☐ Over the Knee
- ☐ Bending Over
- ☐ Lying Face Down
- ☐ Diaper Position
- ☐ _____

I was spanked with a

- ☐ Hand
- ☐ Hairbrush
- ☐ Bath Brush
- ☐ Paddle
- ☐ Wooden Spoon
- ☐ Slipper
- ☐ Cane
- ☐ Switch
- ☐ Belt
- ☐ Leather Strap
- ☐ Tawse
- ☐ _____

Next time I will

_____

_____

Caregiver's Signature _____

Spanking Report

Date _____ / _____ / _____

Today I was spanked by _____

I was spanked because I

_____

_____

What I did was wrong because

_____

_____

I was spanked on my

- ☐ Panties
- ☐ Diaper
- ☐ Bare Bottom
- ☐ Underwear
- ☐ Pull-up

I was spanked

- ☐ Over the Knee
- ☐ Lying Face Down
- ☐ _____
- ☐ Bending Over
- ☐ Diaper Position

I was spanked with a

- ☐ Hand
- ☐ Wooden Spoon
- ☐ Belt
- ☐ Hairbrush
- ☐ Slipper
- ☐ Leather Strap
- ☐ Bath Brush
- ☐ Cane
- ☐ Tawse
- ☐ Paddle
- ☐ Switch
- ☐ _____

Next time I will

_____

_____

Caregiver's Signature _____

Spanking Report

Date _____ / _____ / _____

Today I was spanked by _____

I was spanked because I

_____

_____

What I did was wrong because

_____

_____

I was spanked on my

- ☐ Panties
- ☐ Underwear
- ☐ Diaper
- ☐ Pull-up
- ☐ Bare Bottom

I was spanked

- ☐ Over the Knee
- ☐ Bending Over
- ☐ Lying Face Down
- ☐ Diaper Position
- ☐ _____

I was spanked with a

- ☐ Hand
- ☐ Hairbrush
- ☐ Bath Brush
- ☐ Paddle
- ☐ Wooden Spoon
- ☐ Slipper
- ☐ Cane
- ☐ Switch
- ☐ Belt
- ☐ Leather Strap
- ☐ Tawse
- ☐ _____

Next time I will

_____

_____

Caregiver's Signature _____

Spanking Report

Date _____ / _____ / _____

Today I was spanked by _____

I was spanked because I

_____

_____

What I did was wrong because

_____

_____

I was spanked on my

☐ Panties   ☐ Diaper   ☐ Bare Bottom

☐ Underwear   ☐ Pull-up

I was spanked

☐ Over the Knee   ☐ Lying Face Down   ☐ _____

☐ Bending Over   ☐ Diaper Position

I was spanked with a

☐ Hand   ☐ Wooden Spoon   ☐ Belt

☐ Hairbrush   ☐ Slipper   ☐ Leather Strap

☐ Bath Brush   ☐ Cane   ☐ Tawse

☐ Paddle   ☐ Switch   ☐ _____

Next time I will

_____

_____

Caregiver's Signature _____

Spanking Report

Date _____ / _____ / _____

Today I was spanked by _____

I was spanked because I

_____

_____

What I did was wrong because

_____

_____

I was spanked on my

- ☐ Panties
- ☐ Diaper
- ☐ Bare Bottom
- ☐ Underwear
- ☐ Pull-up

I was spanked

- ☐ Over the Knee
- ☐ Lying Face Down
- ☐ _____
- ☐ Bending Over
- ☐ Diaper Position

I was spanked with a

- ☐ Hand
- ☐ Wooden Spoon
- ☐ Belt
- ☐ Hairbrush
- ☐ Slipper
- ☐ Leather Strap
- ☐ Bath Brush
- ☐ Cane
- ☐ Tawse
- ☐ Paddle
- ☐ Switch
- ☐ _____

Next time I will

_____

_____

Caregiver's Signature _____

Spanking Report

Date _____ / _____ / _____

Today I was spanked by _____

I was spanked because I

_____

_____

What I did was wrong because

_____

_____

I was spanked on my

- ☐ Panties
- ☐ Underwear
- ☐ Diaper
- ☐ Pull-up
- ☐ Bare Bottom

I was spanked

- ☐ Over the Knee
- ☐ Bending Over
- ☐ Lying Face Down
- ☐ Diaper Position
- ☐ _____

I was spanked with a

- ☐ Hand
- ☐ Hairbrush
- ☐ Bath Brush
- ☐ Paddle
- ☐ Wooden Spoon
- ☐ Slipper
- ☐ Cane
- ☐ Switch
- ☐ Belt
- ☐ Leather Strap
- ☐ Tawse
- ☐ _____

Next time I will

_____

_____

Caregiver's Signature _____

Spanking Report

Date _____ / _____ / _____

Today I was spanked by _____

I was spanked because I

_____

_____

What I did was wrong because

_____

_____

I was spanked on my

- ☐ Panties
- ☐ Underwear
- ☐ Diaper
- ☐ Pull-up
- ☐ Bare Bottom

I was spanked

- ☐ Over the Knee
- ☐ Bending Over
- ☐ Lying Face Down
- ☐ Diaper Position
- ☐ _____

I was spanked with a

- ☐ Hand
- ☐ Hairbrush
- ☐ Bath Brush
- ☐ Paddle
- ☐ Wooden Spoon
- ☐ Slipper
- ☐ Cane
- ☐ Switch
- ☐ Belt
- ☐ Leather Strap
- ☐ Tawse
- ☐ _____

Next time I will

_____

_____

Caregiver's Signature _____

Spanking Report

Date _____ / _____ / _____

Today I was spanked by _____

I was spanked because I

_____

_____

What I did was wrong because

_____

_____

I was spanked on my

☐ Panties ☐ Diaper ☐ Bare Bottom

☐ Underwear ☐ Pull-up

I was spanked

☐ Over the Knee ☐ Lying Face Down ☐ _____

☐ Bending Over ☐ Diaper Position

I was spanked with a

☐ Hand ☐ Wooden Spoon ☐ Belt

☐ Hairbrush ☐ Slipper ☐ Leather Strap

☐ Bath Brush ☐ Cane ☐ Tawse

☐ Paddle ☐ Switch ☐ _____

Next time I will

_____

_____

Caregiver's Signature _____

Spanking Report

Date _____ / _____ / _____

Today I was spanked by _____

I was spanked because I

_____

_____

What I did was wrong because

_____

_____

I was spanked on my

- ☐ Panties
- ☐ Underwear
- ☐ Diaper
- ☐ Pull-up
- ☐ Bare Bottom

I was spanked

- ☐ Over the Knee
- ☐ Bending Over
- ☐ Lying Face Down
- ☐ Diaper Position
- ☐ _____

I was spanked with a

- ☐ Hand
- ☐ Hairbrush
- ☐ Bath Brush
- ☐ Paddle
- ☐ Wooden Spoon
- ☐ Slipper
- ☐ Cane
- ☐ Switch
- ☐ Belt
- ☐ Leather Strap
- ☐ Tawse
- ☐ _____

Next time I will

_____

_____

Caregiver's Signature _____

Spanking Report

Date _____ / _____ / _____

Today I was spanked by _____

I was spanked because I

_____

_____

What I did was wrong because

_____

_____

I was spanked on my

☐ Panties   ☐ Diaper   ☐ Bare Bottom

☐ Underwear   ☐ Pull-up

I was spanked

☐ Over the Knee   ☐ Lying Face Down   ☐ _____

☐ Bending Over   ☐ Diaper Position

I was spanked with a

☐ Hand   ☐ Wooden Spoon   ☐ Belt

☐ Hairbrush   ☐ Slipper   ☐ Leather Strap

☐ Bath Brush   ☐ Cane   ☐ Tawse

☐ Paddle   ☐ Switch   ☐ _____

Next time I will

_____

_____

Caregiver's Signature _____

Spanking Report

Date _____ / _____ / _____

Today I was spanked by _____

I was spanked because I

_____

_____

What I did was wrong because

_____

_____

I was spanked on my

- ☐ Panties
- ☐ Underwear
- ☐ Diaper
- ☐ Pull-up
- ☐ Bare Bottom

I was spanked

- ☐ Over the Knee
- ☐ Bending Over
- ☐ Lying Face Down
- ☐ Diaper Position
- ☐ _____

I was spanked with a

- ☐ Hand
- ☐ Hairbrush
- ☐ Bath Brush
- ☐ Paddle
- ☐ Wooden Spoon
- ☐ Slipper
- ☐ Cane
- ☐ Switch
- ☐ Belt
- ☐ Leather Strap
- ☐ Tawse
- ☐ _____

Next time I will

_____

_____

Caregiver's Signature _____

Spanking Report

Date ____ / ____ / ____

Today I was spanked by _____

I was spanked because I

_____

_____

What I did was wrong because

_____

_____

I was spanked on my

- ☐ Panties
- ☐ Underwear
- ☐ Diaper
- ☐ Pull-up
- ☐ Bare Bottom

I was spanked

- ☐ Over the Knee
- ☐ Bending Over
- ☐ Lying Face Down
- ☐ Diaper Position
- ☐ _____

I was spanked with a

- ☐ Hand
- ☐ Hairbrush
- ☐ Bath Brush
- ☐ Paddle
- ☐ Wooden Spoon
- ☐ Slipper
- ☐ Cane
- ☐ Switch
- ☐ Belt
- ☐ Leather Strap
- ☐ Tawse
- ☐ _____

Next time I will

_____

_____

Caregiver's Signature _____

Spanking Report

Date _____ / _____ / _____

Today I was spanked by _____

I was spanked because I

_____

_____

What I did was wrong because

_____

_____

I was spanked on my

- ☐ Panties
- ☐ Underwear
- ☐ Diaper
- ☐ Pull-up
- ☐ Bare Bottom

I was spanked

- ☐ Over the Knee
- ☐ Bending Over
- ☐ Lying Face Down
- ☐ Diaper Position
- ☐ _____

I was spanked with a

- ☐ Hand
- ☐ Hairbrush
- ☐ Bath Brush
- ☐ Paddle
- ☐ Wooden Spoon
- ☐ Slipper
- ☐ Cane
- ☐ Switch
- ☐ Belt
- ☐ Leather Strap
- ☐ Tawse
- ☐ _____

Next time I will

_____

_____

Caregiver's Signature _____

Spanking Report

Date _____ / _____ / _____

Today I was spanked by _____

I was spanked because I

_____

_____

What I did was wrong because

_____

_____

I was spanked on my

- ☐ Panties
- ☐ Underwear
- ☐ Diaper
- ☐ Pull-up
- ☐ Bare Bottom

I was spanked

- ☐ Over the Knee
- ☐ Bending Over
- ☐ Lying Face Down
- ☐ Diaper Position
- ☐ _____

I was spanked with a

- ☐ Hand
- ☐ Hairbrush
- ☐ Bath Brush
- ☐ Paddle
- ☐ Wooden Spoon
- ☐ Slipper
- ☐ Cane
- ☐ Switch
- ☐ Belt
- ☐ Leather Strap
- ☐ Tawse
- ☐ _____

Next time I will

_____

_____

Caregiver's Signature _____

Spanking Report

Date _____ / _____ / _____

Today I was spanked by _____

I was spanked because I

_____

_____

What I did was wrong because

_____

_____

I was spanked on my

- ☐ Panties
- ☐ Underwear
- ☐ Diaper
- ☐ Pull-up
- ☐ Bare Bottom

I was spanked

- ☐ Over the Knee
- ☐ Bending Over
- ☐ Lying Face Down
- ☐ Diaper Position
- ☐ _____

I was spanked with a

- ☐ Hand
- ☐ Hairbrush
- ☐ Bath Brush
- ☐ Paddle
- ☐ Wooden Spoon
- ☐ Slipper
- ☐ Cane
- ☐ Switch
- ☐ Belt
- ☐ Leather Strap
- ☐ Tawse
- ☐ _____

Next time I will

_____

_____

Caregiver's Signature _____

Spanking Report

Date ____ /____ /____

Today I was spanked by _____

I was spanked because I

_____

_____

What I did was wrong because

_____

_____

I was spanked on my

- ☐ Panties
- ☐ Underwear
- ☐ Diaper
- ☐ Pull-up
- ☐ Bare Bottom

I was spanked

- ☐ Over the Knee
- ☐ Bending Over
- ☐ Lying Face Down
- ☐ Diaper Position
- ☐ _____

I was spanked with a

- ☐ Hand
- ☐ Hairbrush
- ☐ Bath Brush
- ☐ Paddle
- ☐ Wooden Spoon
- ☐ Slipper
- ☐ Cane
- ☐ Switch
- ☐ Belt
- ☐ Leather Strap
- ☐ Tawse
- ☐ _____

Next time I will

_____

_____

Caregiver's Signature _____

Spanking Report

Date _____ / _____ / _____

Today I was spanked by _____

I was spanked because I

_____

_____

What I did was wrong because

_____

_____

I was spanked on my

- ☐ Panties
- ☐ Underwear
- ☐ Diaper
- ☐ Pull-up
- ☐ Bare Bottom

I was spanked

- ☐ Over the Knee
- ☐ Bending Over
- ☐ Lying Face Down
- ☐ Diaper Position
- ☐ _____

I was spanked with a

- ☐ Hand
- ☐ Hairbrush
- ☐ Bath Brush
- ☐ Paddle
- ☐ Wooden Spoon
- ☐ Slipper
- ☐ Cane
- ☐ Switch
- ☐ Belt
- ☐ Leather Strap
- ☐ Tawse
- ☐ _____

Next time I will

_____

_____

Caregiver's Signature _____

Spanking Report

Date _____ / _____ / _____

Today I was spanked by _____

I was spanked because I

_____

_____

What I did was wrong because

_____

_____

I was spanked on my

- ☐ Panties
- ☐ Underwear
- ☐ Diaper
- ☐ Pull-up
- ☐ Bare Bottom

I was spanked

- ☐ Over the Knee
- ☐ Bending Over
- ☐ Lying Face Down
- ☐ Diaper Position
- ☐ _____

I was spanked with a

- ☐ Hand
- ☐ Hairbrush
- ☐ Bath Brush
- ☐ Paddle
- ☐ Wooden Spoon
- ☐ Slipper
- ☐ Cane
- ☐ Switch
- ☐ Belt
- ☐ Leather Strap
- ☐ Tawse
- ☐ _____

Next time I will

_____

_____

Caregiver's Signature _____

Spanking Report

Date _____ / _____ / _____

Today I was spanked by _____

I was spanked because I

_____

_____

What I did was wrong because

_____

_____

I was spanked on my

☐ Panties   ☐ Diaper   ☐ Bare Bottom

☐ Underwear   ☐ Pull-up

I was spanked

☐ Over the Knee   ☐ Lying Face Down   ☐ _____

☐ Bending Over   ☐ Diaper Position

I was spanked with a

☐ Hand   ☐ Wooden Spoon   ☐ Belt

☐ Hairbrush   ☐ Slipper   ☐ Leather Strap

☐ Bath Brush   ☐ Cane   ☐ Tawse

☐ Paddle   ☐ Switch   ☐ _____

Next time I will

_____

_____

Caregiver's Signature _____

Spanking Report

Date ____ / ____ / ____

Today I was spanked by _____

I was spanked because I

_____

_____

What I did was wrong because

_____

_____

I was spanked on my

- ☐ Panties
- ☐ Underwear
- ☐ Diaper
- ☐ Pull-up
- ☐ Bare Bottom

I was spanked

- ☐ Over the Knee
- ☐ Bending Over
- ☐ Lying Face Down
- ☐ Diaper Position
- ☐ _____

I was spanked with a

- ☐ Hand
- ☐ Hairbrush
- ☐ Bath Brush
- ☐ Paddle
- ☐ Wooden Spoon
- ☐ Slipper
- ☐ Cane
- ☐ Switch
- ☐ Belt
- ☐ Leather Strap
- ☐ Tawse
- ☐ _____

Next time I will

_____

_____

Caregiver's Signature _____

Spanking Permission Form

Date _____ / _____ / _____

I hereby grant _____

Permission to spank _____

On their

- ☐ Panties
- ☐ Underwear
- ☐ Diaper
- ☐ Pull-up
- ☐ Bare Bottom

Positioned

- ☐ Over the Knee
- ☐ Bending Over
- ☐ Lying Face Down
- ☐ Diaper Position
- ☐ _____

Using

- ☐ Hand
- ☐ Hairbrush
- ☐ Bath Brush
- ☐ Paddle
- ☐ Wooden Spoon
- ☐ Slipper
- ☐ Cane
- ☐ Switch
- ☐ Paddle
- ☐ Leather Strap
- ☐ Tawse
- ☐ _____

Permission Expires   ☐ Never   ☐ _____ / _____ / _____

Caregiver's Signature _____

Spanking Permission Form

Date ____ / ____ / ____

I hereby grant _____

Permission to spank _____

On their

- ☐ Panties
- ☐ Underwear
- ☐ Diaper
- ☐ Pull-up
- ☐ Bare Bottom

Positioned

- ☐ Over the Knee
- ☐ Bending Over
- ☐ Lying Face Down
- ☐ Diaper Position
- ☐ _____

Using

- ☐ Hand
- ☐ Hairbrush
- ☐ Bath Brush
- ☐ Paddle
- ☐ Wooden Spoon
- ☐ Slipper
- ☐ Cane
- ☐ Switch
- ☐ Paddle
- ☐ Leather Strap
- ☐ Tawse
- ☐ _____

Permission Expires   ☐ Never   ☐ ____ / ____ / ____

Caregiver's Signature _____

Spanking Permission Form

Date ____ / ____ / ____

I hereby grant _____

Permission to spank _____

On their

- ☐ Panties
- ☐ Underwear
- ☐ Diaper
- ☐ Pull-up
- ☐ Bare Bottom

Positioned

- ☐ Over the Knee
- ☐ Bending Over
- ☐ Lying Face Down
- ☐ Diaper Position
- ☐ _____

Using

- ☐ Hand
- ☐ Hairbrush
- ☐ Bath Brush
- ☐ Paddle
- ☐ Wooden Spoon
- ☐ Slipper
- ☐ Cane
- ☐ Switch
- ☐ Paddle
- ☐ Leather Strap
- ☐ Tawse
- ☐ _____

Permission Expires   ☐ Never   ☐ ____ / ____ / ____

Caregiver's Signature _____

Spanking Permission Form

Date _____ / _____ / _____

I hereby grant _____

Permission to spank _____

On their

☐ Panties   ☐ Diaper   ☐ Bare Bottom

☐ Underwear   ☐ Pull-up

Positioned

☐ Over the Knee   ☐ Lying Face Down   ☐ _____

☐ Bending Over   ☐ Diaper Position

Using

☐ Hand   ☐ Wooden Spoon   ☐ Paddle

☐ Hairbrush   ☐ Slipper   ☐ Leather Strap

☐ Bath Brush   ☐ Cane   ☐ Tawse

☐ Paddle   ☐ Switch   ☐ _____

Permission Expires   ☐ Never   ☐ _____ / _____ / _____

Caregiver's Signature _____

Spanking Permission Form

Date _____ / _____ / _____

I hereby grant _____

Permission to spank _____

On their

- ☐ Panties
- ☐ Underwear
- ☐ Diaper
- ☐ Pull-up
- ☐ Bare Bottom

Positioned

- ☐ Over the Knee
- ☐ Bending Over
- ☐ Lying Face Down
- ☐ Diaper Position
- ☐ _____

Using

- ☐ Hand
- ☐ Hairbrush
- ☐ Bath Brush
- ☐ Paddle
- ☐ Wooden Spoon
- ☐ Slipper
- ☐ Cane
- ☐ Switch
- ☐ Paddle
- ☐ Leather Strap
- ☐ Tawse
- ☐ _____

Permission Expires   ☐ Never   ☐ _____ / _____ / _____

Caregiver's Signature _____

Spanking Permission Form

Date ____ / ____ / ____

I hereby grant _____

Permission to spank _____

On their

- ☐ Panties
- ☐ Underwear
- ☐ Diaper
- ☐ Pull-up
- ☐ Bare Bottom

Positioned

- ☐ Over the Knee
- ☐ Bending Over
- ☐ Lying Face Down
- ☐ Diaper Position
- ☐ _____

Using

- ☐ Hand
- ☐ Hairbrush
- ☐ Bath Brush
- ☐ Paddle
- ☐ Wooden Spoon
- ☐ Slipper
- ☐ Cane
- ☐ Switch
- ☐ Paddle
- ☐ Leather Strap
- ☐ Tawse
- ☐ _____

Permission Expires   ☐ Never   ☐ ____ / ____ / ____

Caregiver's Signature _____

Spanking Permission Form

Date ____ / ____ / ____

I hereby grant _____

Permission to spank _____

On their

- ☐ Panties
- ☐ Diaper
- ☐ Bare Bottom
- ☐ Underwear
- ☐ Pull-up

Positioned

- ☐ Over the Knee
- ☐ Lying Face Down
- ☐ _____
- ☐ Bending Over
- ☐ Diaper Position

Using

- ☐ Hand
- ☐ Wooden Spoon
- ☐ Paddle
- ☐ Hairbrush
- ☐ Slipper
- ☐ Leather Strap
- ☐ Bath Brush
- ☐ Cane
- ☐ Tawse
- ☐ Paddle
- ☐ Switch
- ☐ _____

Permission Expires   ☐ Never   ☐ ____ / ____ / ____

Caregiver's Signature _____

Spanking Permission Form

Date _____ / _____ / _____

I hereby grant _____

Permission to spank _____

On their

- ☐ Panties
- ☐ Underwear
- ☐ Diaper
- ☐ Pull-up
- ☐ Bare Bottom

Positioned

- ☐ Over the Knee
- ☐ Bending Over
- ☐ Lying Face Down
- ☐ Diaper Position
- ☐ _____

Using

- ☐ Hand
- ☐ Hairbrush
- ☐ Bath Brush
- ☐ Paddle
- ☐ Wooden Spoon
- ☐ Slipper
- ☐ Cane
- ☐ Switch
- ☐ Paddle
- ☐ Leather Strap
- ☐ Tawse
- ☐ _____

Permission Expires ☐ Never ☐ _____ / _____ / _____

Caregiver's Signature _____

Spanking Permission Form

Date ____ / ____ / ____

I hereby grant _____

Permission to spank _____

On their

- ☐ Panties
- ☐ Underwear
- ☐ Diaper
- ☐ Pull-up
- ☐ Bare Bottom

Positioned

- ☐ Over the Knee
- ☐ Bending Over
- ☐ Lying Face Down
- ☐ Diaper Position
- ☐ _____

Using

- ☐ Hand
- ☐ Hairbrush
- ☐ Bath Brush
- ☐ Paddle
- ☐ Wooden Spoon
- ☐ Slipper
- ☐ Cane
- ☐ Switch
- ☐ Paddle
- ☐ Leather Strap
- ☐ Tawse
- ☐ _____

Permission Expires   ☐ Never   ☐ ____ / ____ / ____

Caregiver's Signature _____

Spanking Permission Form

Date ____ / ____ / ____

I hereby grant _____

Permission to spank _____

On their

☐ Panties   ☐ Diaper   ☐ Bare Bottom

☐ Underwear   ☐ Pull-up

Positioned

☐ Over the Knee   ☐ Lying Face Down   ☐ _____

☐ Bending Over   ☐ Diaper Position

Using

☐ Hand   ☐ Wooden Spoon   ☐ Paddle

☐ Hairbrush   ☐ Slipper   ☐ Leather Strap

☐ Bath Brush   ☐ Cane   ☐ Tawse

☐ Paddle   ☐ Switch   ☐ _____

Permission Expires   ☐ Never   ☐ ____ / ____ / ____

Caregiver's Signature _____

Spanking Permission Form

Date _____ / _____ / _____

I hereby grant _____

Permission to spank _____

On their

- ☐ Panties
- ☐ Underwear
- ☐ Diaper
- ☐ Pull-up
- ☐ Bare Bottom

Positioned

- ☐ Over the Knee
- ☐ Bending Over
- ☐ Lying Face Down
- ☐ Diaper Position
- ☐ _____

Using

- ☐ Hand
- ☐ Hairbrush
- ☐ Bath Brush
- ☐ Paddle
- ☐ Wooden Spoon
- ☐ Slipper
- ☐ Cane
- ☐ Switch
- ☐ Paddle
- ☐ Leather Strap
- ☐ Tawse
- ☐ _____

Permission Expires ☐ Never ☐ _____ / _____ / _____

Caregiver's Signature _____

Spanking Permission Form

Date _____ / _____ / _____

I hereby grant _____

Permission to spank _____

On their

- ☐ Panties
- ☐ Underwear
- ☐ Diaper
- ☐ Pull-up
- ☐ Bare Bottom

Positioned

- ☐ Over the Knee
- ☐ Bending Over
- ☐ Lying Face Down
- ☐ Diaper Position
- ☐ _____

Using

- ☐ Hand
- ☐ Hairbrush
- ☐ Bath Brush
- ☐ Paddle
- ☐ Wooden Spoon
- ☐ Slipper
- ☐ Cane
- ☐ Switch
- ☐ Paddle
- ☐ Leather Strap
- ☐ Tawse
- ☐ _____

Permission Expires ☐ Never   ☐ _____ / _____ / _____

Caregiver's Signature _____

Spanking Permission Form

Date _____ / _____ / _____

I hereby grant _____

Permission to spank _____

On their

- ☐ Panties
- ☐ Underwear
- ☐ Diaper
- ☐ Pull-up
- ☐ Bare Bottom

Positioned

- ☐ Over the Knee
- ☐ Bending Over
- ☐ Lying Face Down
- ☐ Diaper Position
- ☐ _____

Using

- ☐ Hand
- ☐ Hairbrush
- ☐ Bath Brush
- ☐ Paddle
- ☐ Wooden Spoon
- ☐ Slipper
- ☐ Cane
- ☐ Switch
- ☐ Paddle
- ☐ Leather Strap
- ☐ Tawse
- ☐ _____

Permission Expires   ☐ Never   ☐ _____ / _____ / _____

Caregiver's Signature _____

Spanking Permission Form

Date _____ / _____ / _____

I hereby grant _____

Permission to spank _____

On their

☐ Panties ☐ Diaper ☐ Bare Bottom

☐ Underwear ☐ Pull-up

Positioned

☐ Over the Knee ☐ Lying Face Down ☐ _____

☐ Bending Over ☐ Diaper Position

Using

☐ Hand ☐ Wooden Spoon ☐ Paddle

☐ Hairbrush ☐ Slipper ☐ Leather Strap

☐ Bath Brush ☐ Cane ☐ Tawse

☐ Paddle ☐ Switch ☐ _____

Permission Expires ☐ Never ☐ _____ / _____ / _____

Caregiver's Signature _____

Spanking Permission Form

Date ____ / ____ / ____

I hereby grant _____

Permission to spank _____

On their

- [ ] Panties
- [ ] Underwear
- [ ] Diaper
- [ ] Pull-up
- [ ] Bare Bottom

Positioned

- [ ] Over the Knee
- [ ] Bending Over
- [ ] Lying Face Down
- [ ] Diaper Position
- [ ] _____

Using

- [ ] Hand
- [ ] Hairbrush
- [ ] Bath Brush
- [ ] Paddle
- [ ] Wooden Spoon
- [ ] Slipper
- [ ] Cane
- [ ] Switch
- [ ] Paddle
- [ ] Leather Strap
- [ ] Tawse
- [ ] _____

Permission Expires [ ] Never [ ] ____ / ____ / ____

Caregiver's Signature _____

Spanking Permission Form

Date _____ / _____ / _____

I hereby grant _____

Permission to spank _____

On their

- ☐ Panties
- ☐ Underwear
- ☐ Diaper
- ☐ Pull-up
- ☐ Bare Bottom

Positioned

- ☐ Over the Knee
- ☐ Bending Over
- ☐ Lying Face Down
- ☐ Diaper Position
- ☐ _____

Using

- ☐ Hand
- ☐ Hairbrush
- ☐ Bath Brush
- ☐ Paddle
- ☐ Wooden Spoon
- ☐ Slipper
- ☐ Cane
- ☐ Switch
- ☐ Paddle
- ☐ Leather Strap
- ☐ Tawse
- ☐ _____

Permission Expires   ☐ Never   ☐ _____ / _____ / _____

Caregiver's Signature _____

Spanking Permission Form

Date ____ / ____ / ____

I hereby grant _____

Permission to spank _____

On their

- ☐ Panties
- ☐ Underwear
- ☐ Diaper
- ☐ Pull-up
- ☐ Bare Bottom

Positioned

- ☐ Over the Knee
- ☐ Bending Over
- ☐ Lying Face Down
- ☐ Diaper Position
- ☐ _____

Using

- ☐ Hand
- ☐ Hairbrush
- ☐ Bath Brush
- ☐ Paddle
- ☐ Wooden Spoon
- ☐ Slipper
- ☐ Cane
- ☐ Switch
- ☐ Paddle
- ☐ Leather Strap
- ☐ Tawse
- ☐ _____

Permission Expires   ☐ Never   ☐ ____ / ____ / ____

Caregiver's Signature _____

Spanking Permission Form

Date _____ / _____ / _____

I hereby grant _____

Permission to spank _____

On their

☐ Panties ☐ Diaper ☐ Bare Bottom

☐ Underwear ☐ Pull-up

Positioned

☐ Over the Knee ☐ Lying Face Down ☐ _____

☐ Bending Over ☐ Diaper Position

Using

☐ Hand ☐ Wooden Spoon ☐ Paddle

☐ Hairbrush ☐ Slipper ☐ Leather Strap

☐ Bath Brush ☐ Cane ☐ Tawse

☐ Paddle ☐ Switch ☐ _____

Permission Expires ☐ Never ☐ _____ / _____ / _____

Caregiver's Signature _____

Spanking Permission Form

Date _____ / _____ / _____

I hereby grant _____

Permission to spank _____

On their

☐ Panties ☐ Diaper ☐ Bare Bottom

☐ Underwear ☐ Pull-up

Positioned

☐ Over the Knee ☐ Lying Face Down ☐ _____

☐ Bending Over ☐ Diaper Position

Using

☐ Hand ☐ Wooden Spoon ☐ Paddle

☐ Hairbrush ☐ Slipper ☐ Leather Strap

☐ Bath Brush ☐ Cane ☐ Tawse

☐ Paddle ☐ Switch ☐ _____

Permission Expires ☐ Never ☐ _____ / _____ / _____

Caregiver's Signature _____

Spanking Permission Form

Date _____ / _____ / _____

I hereby grant _____

Permission to spank _____

On their

- ☐ Panties
- ☐ Underwear
- ☐ Diaper
- ☐ Pull-up
- ☐ Bare Bottom

Positioned

- ☐ Over the Knee
- ☐ Bending Over
- ☐ Lying Face Down
- ☐ Diaper Position
- ☐ _____

Using

- ☐ Hand
- ☐ Hairbrush
- ☐ Bath Brush
- ☐ Paddle
- ☐ Wooden Spoon
- ☐ Slipper
- ☐ Cane
- ☐ Switch
- ☐ Paddle
- ☐ Leather Strap
- ☐ Tawse
- ☐ _____

Permission Expires ☐ Never ☐ _____ / _____ / _____

Caregiver's Signature _____

Spanking Permission Form

Date ____ / ____ / ____

I hereby grant _____

Permission to spank _____

On their

- ☐ Panties
- ☐ Underwear
- ☐ Diaper
- ☐ Pull-up
- ☐ Bare Bottom

Positioned

- ☐ Over the Knee
- ☐ Bending Over
- ☐ Lying Face Down
- ☐ Diaper Position
- ☐ _____

Using

- ☐ Hand
- ☐ Hairbrush
- ☐ Bath Brush
- ☐ Paddle
- ☐ Wooden Spoon
- ☐ Slipper
- ☐ Cane
- ☐ Switch
- ☐ Paddle
- ☐ Leather Strap
- ☐ Tawse
- ☐ _____

Permission Expires   ☐ Never   ☐ ____ / ____ / ____

Caregiver's Signature _____

Spanking Permission Form

Date ____ / ____ / ____

I hereby grant _____

Permission to spank _____

On their

- ☐ Panties
- ☐ Underwear
- ☐ Diaper
- ☐ Pull-up
- ☐ Bare Bottom

Positioned

- ☐ Over the Knee
- ☐ Bending Over
- ☐ Lying Face Down
- ☐ Diaper Position
- ☐ _____

Using

- ☐ Hand
- ☐ Hairbrush
- ☐ Bath Brush
- ☐ Paddle
- ☐ Wooden Spoon
- ☐ Slipper
- ☐ Cane
- ☐ Switch
- ☐ Paddle
- ☐ Leather Strap
- ☐ Tawse
- ☐ _____

Permission Expires   ☐ Never   ☐ ____ / ____ / ____

Caregiver's Signature _____

Spanking Permission Form

Date ____ / ____ / ____

I hereby grant _____

Permission to spank _____

On their

- ☐ Panties
- ☐ Underwear
- ☐ Diaper
- ☐ Pull-up
- ☐ Bare Bottom

Positioned

- ☐ Over the Knee
- ☐ Bending Over
- ☐ Lying Face Down
- ☐ Diaper Position
- ☐ _____

Using

- ☐ Hand
- ☐ Hairbrush
- ☐ Bath Brush
- ☐ Paddle
- ☐ Wooden Spoon
- ☐ Slipper
- ☐ Cane
- ☐ Switch
- ☐ Paddle
- ☐ Leather Strap
- ☐ Tawse
- ☐ _____

Permission Expires   ☐ Never   ☐ ____ / ____ / ____

Caregiver's Signature _____

Spanking Permission Form

Date ____ / ____ / ____

I hereby grant _____

Permission to spank _____

On their

☐ Panties ☐ Diaper ☐ Bare Bottom

☐ Underwear ☐ Pull-up

Positioned

☐ Over the Knee ☐ Lying Face Down ☐ _____

☐ Bending Over ☐ Diaper Position

Using

☐ Hand ☐ Wooden Spoon ☐ Paddle

☐ Hairbrush ☐ Slipper ☐ Leather Strap

☐ Bath Brush ☐ Cane ☐ Tawse

☐ Paddle ☐ Switch ☐ _____

Permission Expires ☐ Never ☐ ____ / ____ / ____

Caregiver's Signature _____

Spanking Permission Form

Date _____ / _____ / _____

I hereby grant _____

Permission to spank _____

On their

☐ Panties   ☐ Diaper   ☐ Bare Bottom

☐ Underwear   ☐ Pull-up

Positioned

☐ Over the Knee   ☐ Lying Face Down   ☐ _____

☐ Bending Over   ☐ Diaper Position

Using

☐ Hand   ☐ Wooden Spoon   ☐ Paddle

☐ Hairbrush   ☐ Slipper   ☐ Leather Strap

☐ Bath Brush   ☐ Cane   ☐ Tawse

☐ Paddle   ☐ Switch   ☐ _____

Permission Expires   ☐ Never   ☐ _____ / _____ / _____

Caregiver's Signature _____

Spanking Permission Form

Date _____ / _____ / _____

I hereby grant _____

Permission to spank _____

On their

- ☐ Panties
- ☐ Underwear
- ☐ Diaper
- ☐ Pull-up
- ☐ Bare Bottom

Positioned

- ☐ Over the Knee
- ☐ Bending Over
- ☐ Lying Face Down
- ☐ Diaper Position
- ☐ _____

Using

- ☐ Hand
- ☐ Hairbrush
- ☐ Bath Brush
- ☐ Paddle
- ☐ Wooden Spoon
- ☐ Slipper
- ☐ Cane
- ☐ Switch
- ☐ Paddle
- ☐ Leather Strap
- ☐ Tawse
- ☐ _____

Permission Expires ☐ Never ☐ _____ / _____ / _____

Caregiver's Signature _____

Spanking Permission Form

Date _____ / _____ / _____

I hereby grant _____

Permission to spank _____

On their

☐ Panties   ☐ Diaper   ☐ Bare Bottom

☐ Underwear   ☐ Pull-up

Positioned

☐ Over the Knee   ☐ Lying Face Down   ☐ _____

☐ Bending Over   ☐ Diaper Position

Using

☐ Hand   ☐ Wooden Spoon   ☐ Paddle

☐ Hairbrush   ☐ Slipper   ☐ Leather Strap

☐ Bath Brush   ☐ Cane   ☐ Tawse

☐ Paddle   ☐ Switch   ☐ _____

Permission Expires   ☐ Never   ☐ _____ / _____ / _____

Caregiver's Signature _____

Spanking Permission Form

Date ____ / ____ / ____

I hereby grant _____

Permission to spank _____

On their

- ☐ Panties
- ☐ Underwear
- ☐ Diaper
- ☐ Pull-up
- ☐ Bare Bottom

Positioned

- ☐ Over the Knee
- ☐ Bending Over
- ☐ Lying Face Down
- ☐ Diaper Position
- ☐ _____

Using

- ☐ Hand
- ☐ Hairbrush
- ☐ Bath Brush
- ☐ Paddle
- ☐ Wooden Spoon
- ☐ Slipper
- ☐ Cane
- ☐ Switch
- ☐ Paddle
- ☐ Leather Strap
- ☐ Tawse
- ☐ _____

Permission Expires ☐ Never ☐ ____ / ____ / ____

Caregiver's Signature _____

Spanking Permission Form

Date ____ / ____ / ____

I hereby grant _____

Permission to spank _____

On their

- ☐ Panties
- ☐ Underwear
- ☐ Diaper
- ☐ Pull-up
- ☐ Bare Bottom

Positioned

- ☐ Over the Knee
- ☐ Bending Over
- ☐ Lying Face Down
- ☐ Diaper Position
- ☐ _____

Using

- ☐ Hand
- ☐ Hairbrush
- ☐ Bath Brush
- ☐ Paddle
- ☐ Wooden Spoon
- ☐ Slipper
- ☐ Cane
- ☐ Switch
- ☐ Paddle
- ☐ Leather Strap
- ☐ Tawse
- ☐ _____

Permission Expires ☐ Never ☐ ____ / ____ / ____

Caregiver's Signature _____

Spanking Permission Form

Date _____ /_____ /_____

I hereby grant _____

Permission to spank _____

On their

☐ Panties ☐ Diaper ☐ Bare Bottom

☐ Underwear ☐ Pull-up

Positioned

☐ Over the Knee ☐ Lying Face Down ☐ _____

☐ Bending Over ☐ Diaper Position

Using

☐ Hand ☐ Wooden Spoon ☐ Paddle

☐ Hairbrush ☐ Slipper ☐ Leather Strap

☐ Bath Brush ☐ Cane ☐ Tawse

☐ Paddle ☐ Switch ☐ _____

Permission Expires ☐ Never ☐ _____ /_____ /_____

Caregiver's Signature _____